Amytis Leaves Her Garden

Poetry by

Karen Kelsay

© 2012 Karen Kelsay. All rights reserved. This material may not be reproduced in any form, published, reprinted, recorded, performed, broadcast, rewritten or redistributed without explicit permission of Karen Kelsay. All such actions are strictly prohibited by law.

ISBN-13:978-0615694023

Cover art "Flora" by Evelyn de Morgan

White Violet Press
1840 West 220th Street, Suite 300
Torrance, California 90501

Foreword

The joy Karen Kelsay evinces in her new book Amytis Leaves Her Garden is real and sustained. A virtuoso of subtle descriptive twists, she carefully chooses each word at its peak of ripeness, then plucks it, so to speak, from the inexhaustible tree of her personal eloquence.

However, whether making a general observation or acknowledging some strand of her own memory and experience, Kelsay remains at all times an astute observer. And what she makes of these small occurrences is neither ordinary nor small. This book consists of fifty subtle and well-constructed poems, all of which may be read and re-read with pleasure, for the beauty of their language and their imaginative force. Karen Kelsay is not only accomplished and prolific; she respects language. In addition, she is also attuned to pleasing the intelligent reader. In this harsh uncaring world, *Amytis Leaves Her Garden* presents an elegant respite; something to enjoy. It is also a testament to a life well lived. Karen Kelsay is a poet to watch.

Sally Cook

"There is a crack in everything, that's how the light gets in."

~ Leonard Cohen

Table of Contents

Winter Lullaby 11
An Evening in May 12
Seaside at Eighty 13
Chain Stitch 14
Remnants 15
Vignette of a Winter Evening 16
Lady of Shalott 17
The Courtship Hour 18
Winter Needlepoint 19
A Beating Wing 20
Sergeant Mockingbird 22
A Proper Man 23
Sorrow's farewell 24
Acceptance 25
At Sunset by the Oak 26
Drawing in the Sheets 27
Quiet Flame 28
Mariana 29
Gathering Moss 30
The Tortoise and the Hare 31
Aurora Speaks to Tithonus 32
Falling in Love with an Old Poet 33
Draining the Cup 34

Princess of Los Algodones	35
Guinevere's Mirror	36
On the British Riviera	37
How to Break a Northern Spell	38
Superchild	39
Outlooks	40
The Drive	41
Suzanne and the Elders	42
Home Decor	43
Photo Prayer	44
Divining a Lost Summer	45
Summer in Italy	46
Footsteps	47
Sara Orange Tip	48
Amytis Leaves Her Garden	49
Lloret De Mar	50
Tumbleweed	51
Aberfan	52
Autumn Ambivalence	53
Damselfly	54
In the Smokey Mountains	55
Acknowledgments	56
About the Author	58

Winter Lullaby

It's always in the violet hour you call,
when dusk spreads infant-smooth across the skies,
and winter teeters on the wings of fall.
The poplars change to gold and improvise.

In spite of chill, the memory of you warms.
Unpunctual star, kind winter brings you near,
to break you from your listlessness—transforms
that vagrant whisper I can barely hear

to incandescent words; the subtle burn
of maple leaves to red, a flame of thought
that gives the seasoned birch a breathless turn,
as random dreams within its twigs are caught.

An Evening in May

I wonder what you're up to, now, my friend.
Does springtime find you nattering away
to bunnies in the yard? Did you attend
the stragglers on that sycamore? Today,

I thought about how often you took walks
beyond the willow, where within the light
thin sunlit rays, like golden-spindled stalks
defined the darkening edges of the night.

White daisies sprang up all around this place,
the lawn seemed rich and full, deep green, but when
a cloud disguised the brilliant Queen Anne's Lace,
the evening's dullness settled in again.

Seaside at Eighty

We'll breakfast at Las Brisas when we're gray,
discussing all our commonalities
and differences, admiring the breeze.
We'll idly chatter on about the way

long rocking eucalyptus branches seem
to hammock threads of morning sun along
the coast. Pale clouds will shift to butter-cream
and melon, swimming through a blue sarong

of tinctured sky. I'll scan the beach and sea
where I once played in tide pools as a child,
then you will say : *The waves are much more mild
on Devon's shore, I really miss Torquay.*

I'll point to where the beach-worn mussel shells
bloom purple, Catalina's outline might
appear beyond the shoals of blue-green swells.
We'll venture forth, oblivious to white

sails cutting southward, tilting toward the shore,
where long ago we bathed and sunned before;
and like two cockle halves worn from the weather,
we'll linger by the oceanfront together.

Chain Stitch

My mother's sewing room has spools of thread
stored on a little wooden rack that's mounted
above her old machine—there're fifty pegs
filled with various colors (I have counted).

Long, loose ends dangle over one another,
frail generations crossing down the wall.
She always puts them back in place when finished:
each signifies a project, large or small,

made of those deeper jewel shades she loves.
And I, a pale blonde daughter, see light-blue
incorporated into her collection,
for pastel dresses she made just a few

decades ago. The pink was for my prom
dress made of cotton taffeta, when nimble
fingers shaped my world, and taught me all
I needed was a pattern, cloth, and thimble.

Remnants

It's such a shame to see the flowers finished,
their blossoms strewn in disarray. All beauty
once tenderly maintained is now diminished,
and caring for it has become a duty.

Forget-Me-Nots I've pressed and dried in pages
watch daisies turn to dust after decay.
For each and every thing evolves in stages,
comes springing up in its due time. Today

I'll search for bulbs once more, reject each stone
between dead stems, wild briar. I'll cradle clay
that knows my touch, my voice, my every bone
and waits for me to name the time I'll stay.

Vignette of a Winter Evening

It's wintertime. The beachfront wears a wrap
of citrus-colored cloud at dusk, and mist
from the Pacific clings to Sago palms.
You are seduced into this lunar tryst,

as moons and endings occupy your mind
of late. Obsession with slow tides, swift gulls,
and balmy surf-scent pulls you to the water,
where rocks across the jetty rise like skulls,

to float above a blackened tide. Your dress
has turned the filmy color of sweet lime.
The moon drops closer, like a ripened fruit.
The emptiness is clear. It's wintertime.

An elegant and arching sky bends near,
hanging like a paperweight, makes pale
promises to fill your darkened void—
yet all the larger landscape wears a veil.

Lady of Shalott

French tapestries, embroidered with spun gold,
hang down against your polished cherry walls.
Around sachets of lavender you fold
soft skeins of yarn. A distant tower calls.
You pause to hear Westminster chimes—a song
that's carried up from Camelot. Light weaves
with shadow near the window pane. A long
alluring ray gleams through the barley sheaves.
Your dress is caught beneath the chair and rips.
You brace yourself to stop the fall, and wield
the loom against the mirror. Your world tips,
dismantled by a knight across the field.
The canvas is in ruins, you're distraught,
and no one else is left but Lancelot.

The Courtship Hour

I love the hour that hangs its weightless haze
of yawn across my bed. An ivory wrap
of humming stillness, spectral dance embossed
in thimble-light. I love the wentletrap

of thoughts and gurgled chants that twist before
white shoals of sleep. The bend and blur of night
with loveliness and brokenness inside
soft vagaries that pivot in the light.

I love the hour subservient to dreams,
when day's satiety leaves remnant sky.
And all beheaded moments shed their wings
into a hushed reluctance as they die.

Winter Needlepoint

Here comes the cold time—holly, pine, and yew,
low grass-laced hills crisscross in winter white;
dark threads of cloud stretch sugar-plum and blue
along a canvas sky of fraying light.

The frost arranges crystals on a limb.
Flakes, falling, reappear as snow on snow
like French knots sewn above the tree root's rim,
that stencil little patterns, to and fro.

The frozen oak is filled with mistletoe,
its yellow berries unconcealed by leaf.
They offer fruit for robin, thrush, and crow.
It makes me think of emptiness and grief—

reminds me of a summer field of yarrow,
and everything that bloomed before the chill.
December brings a tapestry of sorrow,
with knots pulled through a surface of goodwill.

A Beating Wing

Had you but sacrificed one lilac
from an unpruned tree, or smoothed the knotted
curls from my face with your bedraggled hand;

had you but crushed a leaf of lavender
and poured a thimble full of balm into my mouth,
like some elixir

from an ancient land; or sprinkled down
the clumsiest of sighs into my hands.
Had you but arched your eyebrow

like a dying willow branch
across a muddy pond—in one last shade-song
to the minnow near the rocks,

or slipped through untamed gardens
in the august heat, a breath-depriving feat,
without a single rest upon a bluebell rim.

Had you but wrapped your head in orchids,
sung to troubled sky larks without chanting
curses at the bougainvillea thorns—

I would not have to write this verse.
This poem, cobbled up from twisted twigs,
that scrapes the feathered whispers

of my throat. This moulted, metered thing,
that taps inside me like a suffocating wing.
I would not have to listen

to these syllables that parrot out my days
and flap their somberness against
a rib cage of *had yous*.

Sergeant Mockingbird

Between the green and gold brocade of branches,
a mockingbird explores his domicile.
In pale-lit morning of the frayed magnolia
he fans his wing-tips, checks the rank and file

through balustrades and portholes made of twigs.
He eyes the tabby on the wall, takes notes
on where the young retriever sleeps. The flick
and quirk of every sparrow wing denotes

a change of circumstance. He is aware
of his superiority. The cat
looks up as if to say, you are the Sergeant.
Clouds and clotheslines, every fly and gnat

report for duty as he squawks and scans
his daily list of rudimentary plans.

A Proper Man

I like a man straight-laced. The banal kind,
with socks laid out sequentially in drawers.
A man who sorts out problems in his mind
(and leaves them there). Routines and daily chores
are regulated, designated, done.
He never needs a *mommy* when he's ill;
his schedule must come first, before the fun,
no entity derails his stubborn will.
I like a man who reads the fine detail
on lengthy contracts—each hair neatly split.
Who has the super power to curtail
his appetite and works to remain fit.
A man whose principles are always high,
until I tease him with my silken thigh.

Sorrow's farewell

I rest my head on Sorrow's knee
she combs the tangles from my hair
and whispers words, then kisses me—
I sleep, lulled by her dirge-like air.

My dream takes flight to join the birch
that silvery spreads on hill and field;
while moonlight sits upon her perch,
I feel that grief to hope must yield.

I think about eternity—
of spirit worlds in sweet repose;
oh, would I then be sorrow free,
while longing for my loved ones grows?

Then came the morning when I woke,
although my dreams had not revealed
the obscure words that Sorrow spoke—
with her last touch I now feel healed.

Acceptance

Like trees that line a path and intertwine
to form a Roman arch that shades the walk,
alongside which the buttercups recline,
engaged in multi-pedaled flower talk—
so our days are linked in mirth and sorrow,
embracing one another, as they spread,
small buds assure us of a fine tomorrow
by softening dark shadows overhead.
But frigid winds oft come in from the east,
and summer turns away her golden face—
when greenery and blossoms all have ceased,
then only wintry boughs will interlace.

At Sunset by the Oak

I've come into the shadow of the oak
to feel the spine of summer leaves. I've come
to rest in realms of dampness, darkness. Stroke
familiar branches beneath twilight's thumb.
I've come to wrap long vines around my breasts
and smear wet clay upon my dress. To weep.
The nutmeg colored bark becomes a test.
I find my way, I find my way. Time sweeps
me like a leaf across a fieldstone wall,
where like some flightless young, I huddle, cold.
I've never found forgiveness in the small
of night. That human element, controlled
by drifts of tulips and the lilacs' white.
That place I cannot love you in the light.

Drawing in the Sheets

And now, my parents' lives have come to this:
they've taken separate beds. At eighty-four,
my mother's moved into the extra room.
Her dresses line the closet, every drawer

is filled. They've lost their battle with the toss
and turn, the irritating reading light
that singed long shadows into dawn, and all
the sighs of each arthritic night.

A quiet harbinger of change lurks in
the hall, and scribbles words: *Alone, alone*—
and now they heed them following the lines,
before the fates interpret on their own.

Quiet Flame

I read through my old diary tonight.
Inside a sweater drawer is where I found
it—tattered travel log. It had a slight
tear on the spine, but still was neatly bound.
I read my thoughts on some far distant night,
stone turrets wrapped in ivy, summer-crowned
green willow trees with soft Parisian light
across the way. My memory swirled around
each consecrated word, until your name
appeared, a shining brilliance so profound
it burnt the yellowed page with quiet flame.

Mariana

With lowing of the oxen you awake.
And like a crow that's ferried by the moon
across a changeless night into opaque
portholes of sky, your mind is strewn
inside the molding weeds and brambles
of the past. Your farmhouse leans aslant
with age, an edifice that sadly ambles
out an addle-minded creaky chant,
that taints the sparrow-song. Your moated grange,
where even Angelo was overcome
by fields of melancholy, dies. How strange
that dogtooth violets never bloom, and plum
trees wither markedly, their fruit askew
and dim—depression always follows you.

Gathering Moss

You always stopped for no apparent reason,
whenever we walked into town—it drove
me crazy. Every slightest change in season
you'd find a little coppice in the grove,
or see a beetle laboring across
a fallen leaf. I had to break my pace,
transform into a stone that gathered moss.
I couldn't keep annoyance off my face.
And then my knee decided I should learn
to stroll with leisure, letting pain be teacher.
I spotted lilies, pale asparagus fern,
looked up to see the pear tree's every feature.
A faster stride? It almost seems unholy.
How glad I am you still like walking slowly.

The Tortoise and the Hare

It's difficult to figure who'll go first;
mom, with her heart attack, pinched nerve and hip
that wakes her in the night—the chemo drip
still in her veins, or dad, his mass submersed

in slothfulness, who might conceivably
sit in his chair and sink into a coma,
unnoticed, till the dinnertime aroma
would cease to wake him (unbelievably).

My mother swims ten laps a day, hell-bound
to ride her bike at eighty-five. She walks
and chatters constantly. Father seldom talks,
embellishes dessert with cream. The ground

moans beneath his widening girth. My mom
is trim and neat, her sewing room's in order;
dad's office looks like he's a first class hoarder.
The winning post waits like an atom bomb,

or unseen trophy in the 4th dimension.
My father sitting on the couch, no stress,
and mother cooking in her Sunday dress.
I watch the finish line with apprehension.

Aurora Speaks to Tithonus

You are a shadow of your former self,
long suffering has eaten you within.
White-haired and bent, you ask if it's a sin
to be released. If I could wrap myself
around your limbs and carry you like nectar
cupped inside my hands—I'd drink your pain.
You'd float with me at sunup and regain
the will to live. You'll find no holy specter
interceding for you, calling heaven's gods.
No entity excuses you from love
(mine's binding as a tightly buttoned glove).
Here you'll remain against all earthly odds.
The sunrise is a selfish mistress. Stay,
and live with me into another day.

Falling in Love with an Old Poet

I'll never see the intricate small lines,
that years of laughter tallied on his face.
I'll never smooth a tangle from his hair,
or know the ardent way he might embrace
a woman, but it's of no consequence.
I've read his words and touched his intellect.
He died almost a century ago;
it really doesn't matter. I detect
the measure of a man, by wit and passion
the lure is how he wields a phrase. I've been
seduced by someone's lines—the subtle kind
without a mortal body, form or skin.
His intimacies: quiet, aching, daring,
a brimming river ageless and unsparing.

Draining the Cup

After she agonized about the equity
disappearing from her home, and walking away
from the city she grew up in; after she wept
at the thought of leaving white plantation shutters
that slit the morning into little ribbons
of warmth, and the fireplace mantle she had constructed
to look like a picture she found in a magazine—

after she anguished over living in a small apartment
with no garden; after she announced she was taking her piano
with her, no matter what; after she talked to lawyers
and accountants who said there was no logic
in staying—

after she moved into a pint-sized rental
by the beach, and stopped the three hour commute
each day; after she realized a dishwasher for two people
wasted more time than it was worth; after she discovered
her cats got along better in a tiny area; after she could
sleep in, and have an extra cup of tea
before eight o'clock—

after she had no flowers to clip or sidewalks
to sweep; after she spent an hour on the sand and studied
a strip of scarlet cloud that stretched
from Palos Verdes to Santa Monica; after porpoise
appeared and the sun's back-glow turned the bay
into a goblet of rose-colored waves; after she bought
a hot chocolate on the pier and proclaimed it
the best dessert in the world—

She realized how delicious it could be
when the cup is drained.

Princess of Los Algodones

She sits against the fence and holds her cup,
this little beggar girl, of eight or nine.
Her brother picks his toy accordion up;
his music breaks her morning trance. A fine

wrought iron rail collects the trash. I think it's
mixed with prismatic plastic. Aimlessly,
dogs pass screened bakery doors, while light from trinkets
crowns dusty window planters, where I see

Faint ecru-colored roses have become
sun-parched. Unvarying from day to year,
this is her little fairy realm—wild plum
limbs strewn with dirty bulbs, her chandelier.

A tin can madrigal begins to rise
on wind. Black sparrows flit upon command,
like jet-beads scattered in a swift surprise—
or emissaries from another land.

Guinevere's Mirror

And now, she has become like Guinevere.
The shadows of two loves have changed her face.
A vine of bittersweet braids through her halo,
she tells herself, *to love is no disgrace.*

She wears a golden locket with a picture
a second photo's in her jewelry case.
And like expensive balm that brings no solace
her passion and discomfort interlace.

Wrapped up each morning inside good intentions,
disrobed by charm when moonbeams reappear.
Attention from two lovers has its magic.
It's difficult to be a Guinevere.

On the British Riviera

We step across the green onto the promenade
and watch a sloop transition past the harbor of Torquay.
It's late afternoon. Beside me, a German woman
chatters about her retirement and relocation
to the city center. Her husband sleeps

in a hired deck chair, his yellow canvas hat
slanted across his face. Beside a long line of beach huts,
a mother rummages through her bag for coins
and sends her daughter to the ice cream stand.

I trace my finger over your skin, feeling
a raised line between the wrist and thumb—
the only evidence of your twenty-five year
racing career. Its faint glossiness has tattooed

you with your former self, a thin scar
from another era. We marvel at the lack
of waves and watch the sun wedge purple shadows
between rows of white Victorians
near the strand. Trees line the sidewalks

as easterly winds chicane through their fronds.
They remind me of old people, minds rustling
over a sea of yesterdays, waving at tourists
on the British Riviera— each with a story
ridged into their palm.

How to Break a Northern Spell

Remember your expensive basket
of fuchsias the moose ate before sun-up,
and the fat mosquitoes that hovered
around your head when the bedroom lights
went out. Recall how the kids went to school
each morning, beneath street lights
that barely lit the sidewalk. Count the hours
they wouldn't go to bed in the summer
because the sun never left the sky.
Keep in mind the snowsuits
you zipped and unzipped, so the children
could pee every two hours.
Think about the dog and his muddy
kennel, car locks that froze, the Chinook
wind that blew your neighbor's balcony
into your yard. Erase the feel
of static electricity zapping your finger
every time you flicked a light switch.
Imagine the scent of a wet wool blazer.
Pack all those memories
into a tarnished little locket, rub it
like a counter-charm—dig your toes
into the California sand.

Superchild

Alone on the playground's edge,
surrounded by a troupe of invisible ballerinas
who transform her frayed skirt into a flash of tulle

while others play foursquare and hopscotch
on the blacktop, she exercises her superpowers
by blocking out thoughts of her mother's demons.

At night she crawls into bed, waking up alone
in the house at midnight—but nothing frightens her.
A swift cat scratch across her cheek imparts

no sting, she can hold back a decade of tears
with a single squint. Neighborhood children
never hear the words

that wrestle within her head, and even adults
struggle to see evidence of the mother's love
her x-ray vision barely captures.

Outlooks

He drank his booze and climbed the metal ladder
(they always argued savagely, those two).
The roof, his own nirvana—made her madder
when he escaped, inventing jobs to do.
I often thought an ambulance was in
the cards, because of their unearthly shouts.
I wondered if their love had ever been
alive, or if their crazy, violent bouts
had killed it off—until the illness came.
it took away her speech, she couldn't walk
or feed herself. He hovered near, became
a different man, who whispered loving talk
into her ears; and never left her side
but once. (He went up on the roof and cried.)

The Drive

I'm riding in the backseat of the car.
The mountains lift their blue chemise of cloud,
while pre-dawn haze stirs quietly. Bizarre,
how palms along the roadside all look bowed
beneath the desert air. Last night it rained—
mesquites are yellow as a slice of sun.
My parents are in front—I'm self-contained,
my young mind on vacation, watching one
by one, as fresh-washed stars depart. It's been
near forty years since I've been in this seat.
I fold my hands, pretend I'm young again—
not heading to the hospital to meet
white gowns that blend and morph into each other.
My parents chatter on—and I am blind
to fates that whirl and storm above my mother.
This morning I'm the girl time left behind.

Suzanne and the Elders

(the aftermath)

I still undress at sunset like before
when stars decant their hymns of broken light
above the honeyed haze, and orchard lore
lifts pomegranate blooms into the night.

I come to bathe beneath this olive limb,
where oftentimes my prayers are coaxed aloud.
Although this shaded arbor seems a grim
intrusion now, and movements spread a shroud

of thick uneasiness; I enter in
when all the garden gates are closed. My fear
is not recorded like the elders' sin.
I've stoned it, dropped it down to disappear

beneath this pool of water—just like me,
determined not to set my demons free.

Home Decor

I remember sunning on the sand—
My dad in wet-gear rising from the sea,
an air tank on his shoulders, like Godzilla,
throwing off his mask and calling me.
He dragged a mid-sized parrotfish he'd speared,
out of the foam. Its turquoise body flipped
against the beach. I noticed how in minutes
every scale turned ghostly grey, and slipped
from glorious to dull. The taxidermist
restored it to its brilliant, deep-blue self.
Above the sliding door we hung it just
for show. Along a full-length teakwood shelf,
we loaded gemmy doodads from the store.
That handsome fish was hatched for our decor.

Photo Prayer

When cataracts form clouds across my eyes
like fog that settles on the coastal skies
and creaky knees require a wooden cane
to navigate my walk across the lane,
please help me not relinquish vanity
to illnesses or pain. Just swaddle me
in classic silk pajamas, sleek and black,
with little velvet shoes—no flannel sack
to drape around my bones, or pink housecoat
with fuzzy slippers skimming like a boat
across the kitchen floor. I'll take a chain
of gold, Ann Taylor slacks. Let me abstain
from wearing spongy curlers that cause laughs
when children see me in old photographs.

Divining a Lost Summer

I've pushed aside the papers in my tray
and culled the wilted leaves from my bouquet
set on the shelf. I've lit a candle, made
a pot of tea and scones with marmalade,
the kind you liked. The blinds are slit; a cool
north wind has melded palms into a spool
of endive colored fronds. It's quiet here.
I close my eyes; blurred images appear.
The room recedes. I sip the bitter tea
and think about a time by Paignton's sea.
Your gauze-like scent clings to the walls, despair
and giddy memories return. I swear,
I hear a gull and jetty bell's refrain.
They both dissolve like sand hills in the rain.

Summer in Italy

It's been two days since
your chemo session.

We lie together on the bed,
mother and daughter, sinking into
a mattress of memory foam.

Furniture is familiar in this room—
your teak dresser is forty-years old,
and the green lamp still
mushrooms above the end table.
A Mediterranean scene

accents the wall. White sails
splash against summer-blue, terraced homes
rise in the foreground. Two women
link arms by the sea.
You whisper, *I wish I was there*.

Footsteps

I heard you left your garden in Nauvoo
with tufts of flowers fringed in teacup blue

that hemmed wild hyssop you would always miss,
along with china painted with a Swiss

scene on each plate. You gave a hand-stitched quilt
away before the prairie chill could wilt

the daisies by your porch, and left the chair
your husband settled in each night, warm air

immersed in fireflies and prairie clover
all for the Utah valley—starting over.

*

I stack my books against the bedroom wall,
the Persian rug's half-covered by a shawl.

My favorite plates were given to a friend
along with mother's vases. I pretend

I'll never miss the walnut antique clock
or linen dress, my daughter's baby smock

and all the lemons offered by these trees.
In springtime branches swell like gentle seas

with blossoms tinted white as cliffs of Dover.
We'll find another place, my love—start over.

Sara Orange Tip

You could have folded naturally
like a paper triangle, and slipped
into death's pocket—
if you weren't so beautiful.

June's mustard fields and streams
still watch for you. Verbena's purple bloom
has missed your touch. Who captured
you in mid-flight

and pinned you to this board,
forcing you to fly throughout the ages
with your elegance exposed?

Amytis Leaves Her Garden

I left my summer home in Babylon,
where citrine stars, like beveled jewels light
the fields of brittle barley in the night.
I left the terraced temples of the dawn
and plum-soft clouds that fawn the morning hills;
the water lilies, sweet and pregnant flesh
of ruby pomegranates that refresh
long afternoons. I miss the early trills
of songbirds by the stream. There's no return
to shady fig trees arching near the walk,
or mulberries adorned and interlock-
ing overhead. No resting by a fern.
No apple blossom honey by the streams,
or date palm forests waving through my dreams.

Lloret De Mar

My pillow forms a cloud; its corners boast
of jasmine-scented evening's ocean spray.
While closing tired eyes, I drift away
and make my landing on the Spanish coast.
Here, I once walked and swam along the beach;
one night, I caught the rolling moon near France,
and every little starlet I saw dance—
I almost felt they came within my reach.
Remiss of me, with all that's on my mind,
I've tried to push her memory from my head.
She sneaks a wayward whisper near my bed,
and scatters opalescent shells behind.
Before the dawn erases the full moon,
my thoughts of her have all but gone too soon.

Tumbleweed

We are the village, and you are the child
whose mother cares for the senile
man across the way—filling his spare

beds with strung out strangers.
Tumbleweed-girl, with wind-blown hair,
you roll from one neighbor's house to another.

We dress you in pinafores and tie bows
around your pigtails, take you to museums
and ballets—knock on your window

to wake you for school. We feed
you French toast and buy you glittery
barrettes. We are the village,

surrounding the only spark of life
left in a house so crammed with living-dead,
no one can see emptiness.

Aberfan

A russet spire winked through barren trees
then vanished when the sun dulled rusty-red
and filtered over ancient, narrow streets.
Vague visions of the past ran through my head.
I found the chapel on a tiny hill,
long windows held my pensive, solemn stare;
inside, I laid my hand upon a pew,
then thought I heard the echo of a prayer.
Outside, the dusk swirled into thickened clouds
that sent a hush down through the quiet sky;
Old coal slag rose in regiments of green
like altars, to some ancient god on high.
Then winter evening swept each home away,
as darkness covered every lonely place;
and so I never got to hear or see
one laugh or smile upon a Welshman's face.

Autumn Ambivalence

We sit near the stream edge, under the pine's
brittle fingers. Our collective breath
drapes between low branches

like a foggy sheet across autumn's arms.
You spot a black bear in the distance;
I marvel how a sky so blue

can be so cold. Daylight has become
brief, the valley blurred into a ribbon
of frayed leaves. At dusk I see

Denali's shadow from my balcony,
moose eat fuchsias by the backyard deck.
Stalks of rhubarb bend

and twist to earth, breathing
a chilly sigh. No matter how many
winters I greet, this place

will always seem foreign to me.
Everything lies exposed, the beauty
is too vast. God is too near.

Damselfly

Where estuary waters seep into
the muddy shore and wet young willow shoots
along the bay, I caught a damselfly
sequestered near a sycamore tree's roots.

We spoke of rising moons, and how small bands
of stars slip rings of gold around the world
in silent, opalescent sheen that glows,
reflects on watercress—until it's swirled

above the steady song of cricket feet.
And then, a darker note possessed the air,
while silver branches in the grove began
to echo dirges filled with hushed despair.

Warm evening spilled her shadowed dreams, and clouds,
with their relentless, monotonic sigh,
spun quietly across the bank—while we,
like sanctified small angels, hovered by.

In the Smokey Mountains

She was an orchid by a mountain pass,
along an Appalachian trail of blue.
He was a hemlock near the cotton grass,
with crooked branches, needles, limbs askew.
At twilight, they'd admire the dazzling way
celestial bodies filled the void with sparks—
both disillusioned by the glaring day,
unsatisfied with melodies of larks.
She wrapped her leaves around his trunk until
they grew together, some say it was fate.
He kept her shaded for a summer—till
the sky became too heavy of a weight.
By autumn, vines and roots joined in a wreath,
that dried with broken pine cones underneath.

Acknowledgments

Winter Lullaby: *Segullah*
An Evening in May: *The New Formalist*
Seaside at Eighty: *The New Formalist*
Remnants: *Angle Literary Magazine*
Vignette of a Winter Evening: *Angle Literary Magazine*
Lady of Shalott: *Trinacria*
Winter Needlepoint: *Lucid Rythmns; Trinacria; The Hypertexts*
A Beating Wing: *The New Formalist*
Photo Prayer: *14 by 14 Magazine*
At Sunset by the Oak: *Fire in the Pasture anthology*
Drawing in the Sheets: *Toasted Cheese* (Best of the Net nomination)
Quiet Flame: *String Poet; Exponent II*
Mariana: *Mezzo Cammin*
The Tortoise and the Hare: *Verse Wisconsin*
Aurora Speaks to Tithonus: *Trinacria*
Draining the Cup: *Fire in the Pasture anthology; The Boston Literary Magazine*
Guinever's Mirror: *Trinacria, Fortunate Childe Publications*
On the British Riviera: *Flutter Poetry Journal; Wilderness Inteface Zone*
How to Break a Northern Spell: *Fire in the Pasture* anthology
Superchild: *Thick With Conviction, Fortunate Childe Publications*
Outlooks: *String Poet*
Diving a Lost Summer: *The Pennsylvania Review; Fire in the Pasture*
Summer in Italy: *Pirene'sFountain*
Sarah Orange Tip: *Flutter Poetry Journal*
Amytis Leaves Her Garden: *The Flea*
Acceptance: *The New Formalist*—from the e-chapbook "Somewhere Near Evesham"
Autumn Ambivalence: *Triggerfish Critical Review; Flutter Press*
Damselfly: *Trinacria; Willow's Wept Review*

Aberfan: *The New Formalist* from the e-chapbook *"Somewhere in Evesham"*
A Proper Man: *Trinacria*
Footsteps: *Hudson View; The HyperTexts*
The Courtship Hour: *Foliate Oak; Trinacria* (Pushcart nomination)
Gathering Moss: *Mezzo Cammin; The Touch: Journal of Healing*

The Following poems appear in the book *Dove on a Church Bench* (Punkin House Press 2011), and are reprinted with the permission of the publisher: *Amytis Leaves Her Garden* and *The Courtship Hour*

About the Author

Karen Kelsay, native of Orange County, has been widely published over the past five years in poetry journals and anthologies. She is the founder of *Aldrich Press* and *Alabaster Leaves Publishing*, two small presses that publish mid-career poets. Her poetry has been nominated five times for the Pushcart Prize, and Best of the Net. She recently received the Fluvanna Prize (2012) from *The Lyric* (the oldest magazine in North America in continuous publication devoted to traditional poetry), has been featured in *The New Formalist* and spotlighted in *The Hypertexts*. She was recently interviewed at *The Poet's Corner* with Russell Bittner, and at *A Motley Vision* (an award winning blog devoted to exploring Mormon literature, criticism, publishing and marketing — plus film, theater, art, music, and pop and folk culture). Five of her poems have been included in the anthology: *Fire in the Pasture: 21st Century Mormon Poets*, which is comprised of eighty published Mormon poets from the past two decades—the first book of its kind in twenty years. Her most recent full length book, *Dove on a Church Bench* (Punkin House Press 2011), was followed by *Lavender Song* (Fortunate Childe Publications 2011). She is the editor of the online poetry and art journal, *Victorian Violet Press*, and lives in Torrance, California with her British husband and two cats.

www.ingramcontent.com/pod-product-compliance
Lightning Source LLC
Chambersburg PA
CBHW070519090426
42735CB00012B/2839